Refuel your Heart...
journal belongs to...

© 2017 Ranch House Press
All rights reserved. Printed in the United States of America.

www.annettebridges.com

ISBN: 978-1-946371-19-5

www.ingramcontent.com/pod-product-compliance
Lightning Source LLC
Chambersburg PA
CBHW051252110526
44588CB00025B/2967